Other books by Edward Kleinschmidt:

Magnetism, The Heyeck Press
    Bay Area Book Reviewers Poetry Award for 1988

First Language, University of Massachusetts Press
    Juniper Prize for 1989

To Remain, The Heyeck Press
    Gesu Poetry Award for 1990

Works and Days, University of Pittsburgh Press
    Winner of the Associated Writing Programs Poetry
    Contest, to be published in Fall 1999

Bodysong

The Heyeck Press: Woodside

BODYSONG

Love Poems by

Edward Kleinschmidt

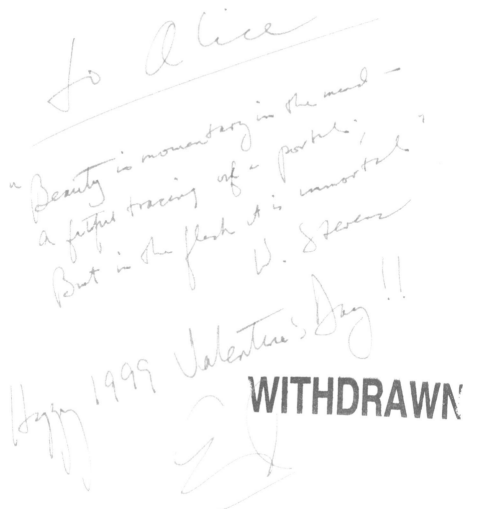

To Alice

"Beauty is momentary in the mind —
a fitful tracing of a portal;
But in the flesh it is immortal"
W. Stevens

Happy 1999 Valentine's Day!!

We are grateful to the editors of the following
journals and anthologies in which these poems,
some in earlier versions, were first published:
*Antioch Review, Apalachee Quarterly, Bottomfish,
College English, Hawaii Review, The Journal, The
Little Magazine, MSS, Mississippi Mud, North
Dakota Quarterly, One Meadway, The Pennsylvania
Review, Poet & Critic, Poetry, Poetry Northwest,
Razzmatazz, Yellow Silk; Mixed Voices: Contempo-
rary Poems about Music,* Milkweed Editions,
*Concert at Chopin's House: A Collection of Polish-
American Writing,* New Rivers Press.

Thanks go also to the Virginia Center for the
Creative Arts and The MacDowell Colony,
where several of these poems were written.

The Heyeck Press
25 Patrol Court, Woodside CA 94062 USA
www.heyeckpress.com

for F.E.N.M.

Assunta Primavera

My lips
move
as you
read me

Contents

First Kiss

Front seat, you, me, the 1969 Volvo
revving off its tachometer, the needle almost
asking us how long it can redline, and our
noses, lips, eyes, tongues, auto parts, private
changed to public parts, our republics joined by
edict, your southern republic for which *this*
stands, your fingers around the wishbone, the

Moment the foam is on the wave, the orchidity,
always the slide trombone playing the hallways, the
y of you, the I.O.U., the full throttle, rain in sheets,
exhale, rocking horse, first kiss, licked luck, purrs,
stripped, sheet lightning, this is how long we can last.

Passion on the Pullman

The train tracks
make our cries shatter
and crack the glass

around our hearts.
The rhythm of the rocking
car plays counterpoint

to your bass and my treble.
Hey porter, cancel
our dinner reservations.

We'd rather stay and eat
with our fingers. We
are tied to each other

and our grapes are about
to burst. Rouse us in
the morning if we are not

already up. Tell us
if our whistle is
too loud, or if you need

another engine over
the Great Divide. We
will tell you when we

come swaying and tipping
down the tracks, when we
come to the river, when
we come out of this tunnel.

Quodlibet

Whatever you will do with the indefinite art-
icle *a* will please me, a hot breath
between your lips.

　　　　　As in the hayloft last May,
the bales coming apart, the night of that
day, the staying up until we lost
count of the times.

　　　　　The rhymes here
are in my head, on my tongue,
longing for your scheme, song being
always sung, drum of sound within
you coming clearer.

　　　　　Your only cry,
your *What You Will*, your bill for
happiness being continuously
paid, joyfully said in lines
ten times longer.

　　　　　We are folded in
an envelope of sheets. We are photos
expertly exposed, clay vases handily
turned. Your lips are sculpted by
the tips of stars.

　　　　　And tonight when
the bed is still and always warm, Edward will.
And you will. You are future, you are present
perfect. You will do. Will. Do.

Without Thinking

You are as smart as the cherries that change
back to pale when they're about to be picked
and fall from their tree weeks later, darker
and untouched. You know how to spell
rain, misspell it into torrent, flood, disaster.
You know words as long as your fingers.
The towel usually wrapped around your head
to soak the sweat from all this work is
hissing on the radiator. You've trained
the dog to train the cat to train the mice,
who really *do* need training, who are ready
at all moments to chew through the legs of
the King's Chair. You want to train them
to bring the crown to you. When you were two,
you threw your dish out the window with enough
spin it became the moon that day, then
flew back to you. If you were dead today,
you would not be as dead as most. What
is the cost of being alive? Something multiplied,
something divided, something subtracted, nothing
added. Each time you think to yourself you
lose a minute of immortality, a thing the rest
of us think is not important enough to die for.
First you thought love, love. Now, once again,
you think love. This is not difficult for
you to imagine, it is leaves on and leaves off
trees, it is simply looking out the windows,
windows all around only open always.

Possibilities of Love

We are left open and wet like shells young
girls string on strips of kelp and wear
around their necks and wrists and ankles into

the sea. In the washed-over sand, we
have to imagine our names were there, in
silver, your name like a rabbit, like

your feet, that turn away from me after
dark nights soften our bodies, turn
them into deep pools of water, fresh water

cupped in our hands on these hot beaches,
the sun which hardens us, our hair
like field straw, but it is our soft grass,

we nest in it and each other. And our hands
keep building, like a stonemason sleeping:
buildings he has never been in want his hands

again. It is you I want again, left open.
Now somewhere else, out of reach of my brown feet,
my shell that has escaped into love, my name.

And you are here, now with pearls in your
hair, and I want to dive to find you
and carry your pearls up to air between

my lips. And to hear you breathe in
as if you were breathing for the world
and will never stop. I sleep on a dune

as if on an animal waiting to carry me down
these beaches to you. And I cannot think of
a letter that is not in your name. And I cannot

think of your arms without my own wet and
stretching out. And I cannot dream of your eyes,
without them, right now, looking closely into mine.

I Hear Frances Singing

I am in my
  right place
none other, no green
  or any other
color would do,
  does. This
night when the roof
  shook with
lightning and heat
  I threw off
old covers, left
  my prints
on the wooden floor.
  This was easy.
This was going
  through thick
air like history. I
  found you in the
bathtub, white skin
  on white porcelain,

reading, what you do
  from the inside
out. The light from one
  candle made a
mirror of me to
  you. You looked
and looked, brushed
  aside the steam,
the dark corners. The
  water is the same
as the room, you said,
  the same as the sheets,
the bed was rocking with
  heat and you are
reading, letting the water
  slide out from under
you, turning the right
  handle back on and
the room fills up with that
  sound. I get in.

Big Talk

Move over, shove
off. I'm feeling
violently opposed
to any reconciliation.
Rip the seams out and
start over. I'm taller,
bigger than the last
and I want you to know that.
I didn't ride in from
Nebraska on a scallop
shell. My feet have
wings and these wings fly.
Of all the trees in
this land, I know
what's on top. I don't
read late news, I make new.

Around the table is food
and the food doesn't
know who I am so I'll
eat and eat and eat.
I dream. And last night
I played the piano
before hundreds without
knowing notes, and I unlocked
those keys. I've got my feet
on the ground and not
the other way around
and I eat dirt and howl
at the moon, after
dinner, after everything.
So. Is there some way
you can take me into your heart?

Remembering Sweet Lives

We use persimmons
as impossible magnets
and blow on
each other's hot coals:
Hallelujah! This is

the coming down
of the rain. This is
the season of no lack
of twirling lights, hanging
gloriously on the trees,

children-colored in the sun.
I want to mention
here the brilliance.
We all see it happening
too late and again

when something flies
in our minds with the green
wind and the trees
on fire, and the ground
underwater.

Overloaded, you might have
said again, dreaming.
Put all on me.
I am a statue,
a vision, a hill

already covered with trees.
I believe in spontaneous
combustion. It happened
to my grandfathers
their whole lives,

but they used
the river wisely.
I can still see them,
once anonymous
as sticks, now always

on the verge, their
skin shiny, their
laughter telling that
over the mountains
is more, but more of

the same. This was again
the turning point. I felt
my veins fill
like flumes in spring.
I jumped up

and shouted, *Keep.*
You said, *If
you want to shout,
I'll give you something
to shout about.* You

did. And I am:
inventing another formula.
If there is an
explosion in all this,
it is us.

Bad Dreams

Go to bed quietly now. Now
you can dream towns of opals,
tangerines, fires, tile floors.
Dream on the inside of your
body no one except me

knows. Forget about him,
his shoes scraping the side-
walk, or his written
curses in the wet cement.
Forget his banging on all

doors of the house in turn.
His remembering that only
the good can walk through.
These are machine-age
ghosts. Find the right

switch and they're gone,
power off, no more grinding
and pulling levers all
night. Think of nothing
at all, or dream only of the next

open field that will continuously
remain open, the next ocean.
Dream of stone walls, too—
and forget damage, dream
love, dream the first person plural.

Bodysongs

Let me pull the string:
I love to watch the silk slide
over your nipples.

Walked around the house
today: hardness at full mast:
Come: I need your breath now!

You call for the third
time this afternoon: and I
answer, cradle the receiver.

Stopped wearing under-
wear: too expensive to replace
all those you've ripped off me.

Which lips do I like better?
The ones I see every day or
the ones I see every day?

Use both hands to take
me in—use your hips to
keep me there: there, there, there.

❖

This morning the largest
hardness hardly could fit
you. You filled me.

❖

Who has the longest
finger for the right job: hire
me: I work overtime.

❖

Your wet lips just got
wetter. I've been watching them
up close. This close. Close.

❖

Lick *here,* you say, and
I lick here: lick *there* you say
and I lick there.

All day my nipples
have missed your nipples. They rise
when yours rise: one wave.

❖

That pillow you put
under you to arch us: now
it gives us double dreams.

❖

The cats in the garden
jump over us, smell us: haven't
they seen such nakedness before?

❖

The first time: the blue pool:
our bodies joined and weightless,
souls floating to the surface.

❖

Bring out the abacus:
the beads click, click, click, the thousand
times now we've made this love.

I want to whisper a
recipe in your ear: take
one of these, take two of these . . .

Speak into my microphone:
can't you feel the feedback up
your back: *re-ver-ber-a-tion?*

Your lovely round pink wet
licked nipples connected to
the licked bud down below.

The doctor said: take one
before bed, one when you arise,
one now, one later.

All day we did it:
the Jade Gate opening the night.
What great aches, great love!

You smell your hand after
I've come to find out where we came from:
the ocean. The string of pearls around
your neck now wound around me, to make me harder
still, harder moving, the wave inside you.

Where hardness meets wetness:
here, grab this bedpost:
here, hold on to these:
here, make me disappear:
here, you are what I want.

Aphrodisiac

Sex is abstract:
Let me show you.

Hard Sell: Valentine

Explosions are always
ten miles deep. I
don't always know how to

think that way. But what I
should say is *I mean.*
And what I do say

is what doesn't matter.
Anyhow, cancel this
hard sell and if you

can't and continue to
think and paint black
stripes to simulate mental

prison, I say let me out,
let me go home down
the dark dirt road and talk

to all the dust devils
wanting a ride in my
station wagon, making

one last stop next
to your heart, your
pumping red heart.

All right, I'll give you
this: picture this: a wrist-
watch on a table top, a talking

book with a Southern accent,
two goats who joke,
a bathtub of ice cream,

a green eye, clean
sheets, a feather fan,
a dancing man, someone

to tell you the time
and the place, and if
you want: love.

Horoscope

You're sexy
and always will be.
Memory

doesn't stop you.
Beware of gratitude
from unlikely people who

ask advice.
Order your scotch without ice.
Tighten the vise

of love. Portray
all of your future in your grace.
Obey

no
one. If you're in tow
cut the line. Float.

Love's License

We have licked time off each other's bodies,
sliding under the covers of our fifteenth spring.
Outside, plum blossoms cover the curves of
late model cars. The seams of baseballs twist
in oiled gloves. We have love insurance
when we're driving, driving, being driven, minute
by minute payments, day and night emergency
service, free towing. But our love hasn't any
accidents we didn't invent ourselves, the puzzle
with the last irregular piece found, clicking
now into place, all the looks on loan and overdue
from the love library. We've had a paint job, then
the hand wax job, glass rubbed and rubbed. We
are ready to go again and again, throw the speedometer
through the window, feel the entire duration of
during, the right before, the right after, the long
after, the long before, the foreplay, the play
ground, the green yellow red, the long
drive home, the reclining bucket seats, the shaking
car, the tickets and tickets and tickets we've
gotten, we've given, the left blinker flashing,
forever in that fast, left lane.

Anonymous Love

Call it what you will, what you can, what you
imagine its name to be. A phenomenon whose time
has come. It has lived at all the addresses
you've forgotten, has been dropped overboard
with empty cans of beer, has been set
conspicuously on hot car seats. If you
could call it and it would hear you,
it would come. You write *Renaissance,* and
sign your name to it. Autograph the moon
if you like. No one's looking. The engine idles
and the top's down as far as it will go. Love's
the Anglo-Saxon word you trip on—hurdle
the *L,* roll over the *o,* slide under the *v,*
and around the *e.* Your name's in all the books.

Apricots and Figs

The wind through the fine wire screen
scatters finely over us who only seem
to mind. Like wild ribbons we have wrapped
each other's bodies in this room, cream-
and chocolate-colored, on this bed, draped
like a fountain, centered in us. We have seen
what thickness love is. We have climbed ladders
to touch the young figs and be touched by them.
The tree shakes, this one apricot, and scatters
fruit. All stars come out in trees and every stem
is heavy with confusion of itself attached, then
unattached and free. The fig loves the apricot.
More of each come showering the bed, all opened
and flaming with a delight that never stops.

The Sympathetic Nervous System

It seems to understand always
that the only place for a man-

to-woman talk is in private,
in hiding, crouching behind crates

of apples and peaches yet to be
opened, eaten. This system, in order to see,

has use of our eyes, is partial to a good
look. That's well understood.

Spontaneity, though, does serve
itself. The lurch, grab, swerve,

curve, and jab are not for
the relaxed, the laid-back, the floored.

Kick our legs out, it tells us,
dance while the dancing is good. Lust,

be lively, extrapolate, be late
if we've always been early, celebrate

the news and lack of it, that
we live—with all our times and cats

and sit-down strikes and roller-
coasters, trips to coasts, stolen

glances, honey-making schemes,
cream in the coffee, scenes

of romance, kissing, kissing,
kissing, kissing, kissing, kissing, kissing.

The system might remind us that the 8th
kiss without a break could make

us suffocate our love: "Go easy."
The system, however, will do what it pleases:

which are truly wonderful things!
For example: it tells time, rings

when we've had too much, grabs hold
of real love, real sex, not some cold

passion of want or need because
we haven't got or don't give. Applause:

that's what we need to feed this system:
and each other's lips, that we need to kiss them.

Discovering the Yellow House

We dreamed often of the yellow house.
It was in the middle of the highway

being hauled away. The broken dishes
in the cupboard started speaking

Chinese. The highway emptied into
a whirlpool created by our minds

swirling in the body of our bed.
Now we are hiding under other dreams:

in the middle of the house
is a vase with four poppies,

each discovering its own direction.
They are red and singular. They grow

larger, as if blooming in the minds
of old painters. They spin with

four petals like wheels of fire—
and all the rooms catch the signal,

the alarm to change, to change into fire.
The sun isn't dying, it's whirling.

It will set you on fire and leave only
your shadow. And all the fish in

the black pond simply swim by copying
their reflections. So our dreams

copy the dreams of the yellow house:
the one of the house empty for 100 years,

for 200, and 300 years. The doors still
opened and closed regularly. It received

offers for sweepstakes and insurance
but seldom responded. It watched clouds

form most days and during the winter hid
the sun in the basement, next to the jars

of apricots and yellow beans. It stayed
healthy, stopped subscribing to

the paper, kept its cats clean and
spiders calm and its windows desirous.

Pastorale: Anniversary

We walk in plaid fields where
the children played and give each other
long plumes to reach the cherries.
The tree trunks rub our knees and thighs,
send sparks down our wet limbs by the handful,
our hands full of red fruit twice ripe to cracking.
White peace seeps deep in our skin,
and body shadows lay soft moss in damp places.
When our backs arc, we resurrect ruined aqueducts:
rough-hewn rocks cool with moving water.
When we move, we interpret motion as sound.
We are there, and there it's over us, and all over us.
We are not forced by some rural rule.
When the cold wind comes up, we may remove our clothes,
and hand print the grasses with our news.

Sex

Yes, we've had duplex-sex, this couple that we are,
we're architects of sex, and the sect we've formed is sex,
all the dialects in our country speaking the same word,
and the beds are big blank checks of sex, and when
we think unidentified flying objects we think space-sex,
and if the weather in the room is bad we give
rainchecks, and when we've gotten to the bottom of
the box of Kleenex we think no-pain, no-gain-sex.
And if what was unaroused now suddenly resurrects—
then sex. And then you flex sex: no sex perplex here,
just rub rub rub that cerebral cortex and magic: great
sex. Sex is flux, you've said, sex in châteaux, bundled
in Gortex, sex in Texas, sex after doing income taxes,
but never faux-sex or phone-sex or hoax-sex or hex-sex or
anticlimax-sex. But apex-sex, vortex-sex, cost-of-living-
index-sex. And the after effects of sex: no side effects
(except love), but great phoenixes circling the bedrooms,
filling the air with Vitamin B complex and climax, sound
of sixty saxes all in tune, and all the glass shattering, even
the Pyrex: playing only-connect-sex, pluperfect-sex, sex-sex.

Magnificent Romance

We love! When the skies
are night and the cats
are night. When the moon

wears long white dresses and
dreams across its own surface.
When May wins the race

for 2002, and January,
sweet faced January, cheers.
When the clouds disappear,

or reappear, to turn to pears.
When the dance is always
slow! When the gauges

are in the red and the lights
are all on and blinking. When
we rise pan-architectural,

spireless, out of breath,
Romanesque, when we, whole and
Baroque and mirrored, when we,

high and climbing and diving
and all, all the colors.
When the ocean rolls backwards.

And when the elephants
from all the lands are
in the same clearing and

the ground is shaking around
and around and when we too
go around and go around.

Bodysongs

First it was you then me &
then it was me then you & then
it was you then me & then it was
me then you & then it was
me then me & then it was you then me
& then it was you then you.

❖

The dark wine in your
mouth is now in my mouth:
we are the only bottle we need to open.

❖

I follow the lines
your lips make on me, your
lips which hold me tight.

❖

Later we laugh at the telephone
you threw through the third story
window, smashed black plastic on
the sidewalk—how dare
it ring while we're making love.

You are the bee, wings brushed
against my pollen as you
move deeper into the flower,
find where the sweetness is.

After the third time, you fell
asleep before me: the knockout
drops in your full glass of water.

I would ring you up before
I come: but we always have
the phone off the hook.

❖

Five o'clock: Morning?
Afternoon? We're rubbed raw, whatever
it is the hands say.

❖

Tongue-lash me, pull
hair, hum the right hum
in my left ear: I'm yours.

After carpet burn, after
sliding on cold kitchen tile:
I'm ready for a bed.

❖

On your back I write
I love you with my breath
over and over, over and over.

❖

This is blood's best
use: that it can harden
certain things it touches, that
it can make you wonderfully blush.

❖

You slip in the bath
with me: the water turning hotter,
hottest, the hot waves capsizing us.

Pass me
your body

I feel enormous today!
Without you to see me
so naked, who am I?

All day I've heard the rain
on our bodies: we cover ourselves
with each other and love seeps through.

I lick love letters
on your breasts. Can you guess
what they spell? You, who
have hold of my best pen,
you, who can make *it*
write everything.

Whose body is this:
Yours? Mine? This part yours,
then mine. This part mine, then yours.

On the double bed: rub
On the queen-size: scream
On the twin bed: sin
On the king-size: cling
On the chaise longue: tongue
On the kitchen counter: mount
On the throw rug: hug
In the back seat: great!
On the boat dock: rock
In the back room: swoon
On the back porch: more!
In the hallway: sway
In the hammock: suck
On the surfboard: lord!

Cooking to Music

"Are we going to measure or are we going to cook?"
Simone Beck

The day pounds hard against our temple doors,
and our skin is as taut as the high breath
of a Chinese kite. We considered rolling off
each other's tongues like Italian. We told

the cook to cook, that we've come with all
the ingredients. We've churned new butter
in our newer bodies. This is no trick, this
handling hot coals on our tongues. And feel

these young fruits, put your nose close
to the full basket. The strawberries pull
open like red silk purses. Slice the ripe
cheese deeply. We are thick with our love.

We scatter orchids and apples around
the piano and catch their singing
fragrance in our strings. We are twin cellos
strummed and rising in a saraband.

Play on, play on, play on, play on, play on.

The Next Day

The maples in the back yard
haven't changed colors. They're
still against blue. We love the hand
shaped leaves. At night, we stay up,
take walks to the cemetery, watch

them unload shadows from the back
of a truck. Shadows from strangers
in Montana, shadows from war orphans
in Honduras, and the mental wars
of Greenland. Will the best of us

have the warm graves? Should we find
someone now to sweep off our gravestones
after the storms? We laugh together
running home. I promise to cut your
fingernails when you die. I promise

to prick you hard with a sharp pin,
my mortal, and color your lips and mine
the shade of your deepest blood. As I leave

you, I'll toss your nails in the air and they will
hang there for a moment, all the moons in

eclipse. Right here, do the moths want desperately
to come into your rooms, into your light?
This California light, you say, and I hear
you say it, is of black squirrels eating
guavas, is of the delta of salt water, is

of the redwoods holding out the blue. Yesterday
we held the dried red pepper to that light.
And each time we love, one more pepper
in a field in Salinas dries up, is ours, gives
us fire, its seeds, all the rooms inside

to turn red in, to make even the water burn.
In autumn, I am not too practical. Do you
think I think in circles, incestuous circles,
my sister, my circe? Change me into
something. Change me into someone I am.

Your Tongue

What a tongue
that comes out
between

your lips.
I would give
whatever you

want. I do speak
your languages:
tongue and groove,

apricot wainscoting,
butter and cream
on the kitchen table,

the one I want to
go under with you.
We will strip off

the tablecloth. We are
magicians. We make
things disappear, then

reappear, disappear, then
reappear, all night long.
But this tongue, love,

I have got to have it.
To trace the map
of my body, the inroads,

rugged terrain, back
alleys, wilderness areas.
The tip of your tongue

is the tip of a
world. I want
to see it all.

When and Where I Am Visualized

On the street corner where
they bend the bow over

the tight strings and plink
plink above the bus roar.

When a pailful of pennies
swishes by unannounced, different

from dimes, more like coffee in
a tin cup, the reflection of

someone else's face. At the drugstore
with cold cream and hot lather. At

the produce stand, minding the apples,
or at Frances's kissing the narcissus

full on its mouth. Showering
is a slow dance. Shaving, I

start to appear. I roll in cotton
and am suddenly dressed. Or

when I say yes! the quartet,
which is saying yes! to whomever

they are playing. Or playing
at being serious, going to a party

of words. When death is a
metal I can swallow, and

will solidify, and there I
am, hardened, shiny underneath.

How You Continually Come as a Surprise

You advance. You approach the speaker:
you advance in a very specified manner.

You arrive, having moved and made
progress. You reach a point—this

is the result of order. You appear
to occur in time. You arrive to end.

Come to an understanding in one
of your particular positions. You say

the bus came to an abrupt halt or, reaching
further, hair comes to the waist. You

prefer to exist at a particular point
or place like the letter *T* coming before

U. How did it happen? How did you come
to know that? If this is simply the result,

this comes of your carelessness. It may
fall into the mind: the idea might come

to you. The study of your background,
is the project coming along well?

Do you ever experience orgasm like a
knot coming loose? If you are available,

are you obtainable? Do you come in two
sizes? If this really turns out to be,

would you say your wish came true? But
come now, this is enough! I don't want to

criticize you, to wear you through like cloth.
Come what may, I propose to remain here.

I'm recovering. I want to anchor here awhile.
I believe our plans will be settled come Friday.

Excitement

Too loose, your clothing,
head of ivory, hands of
Italian marble, veined and
cool. It's the wool itch,
the thrust of the engine
around the corners, on our
way to hot sand, sweating
on the beach. Your arms like
snakes around my neck, my wrists.
The steering wheel rotating like
the dial on the telephone—you know
where to reach me—at home,
when to reach me—at all times,
how to reach me—with your heart,
with your lips, with your eyes.
You're capable of it always,
the great *it* of love. *Like* is
a tree easily climbed, we'll
stay up for awhile or keep
climbing. *Love* is the channel

we cut when the drifting down together
takes its own unusual course.
Will the ocean take our clothes
away like we take each other,
the steady beating wave, the curl,
the foam? The fresh and the salt,
the chair for making love in,
the bed for resting afterwards,
the hummingbird's tongue longer than
its body, the bee's stinger, the wet
sticky loamy spume of leaves, of
hay, of making hay, of love.
We trust the truest tongue will
circle its mark, will not hesitate
to delay the best words
spoken, touching the right spot,
not too much to ask, to
scream and beg for, to coyly
intimate, to flatly say yes.

Say So

Meaning that I love you, your repetition,
your back arched, mouth open to me,
that your hands can untie the tight
laces of my body, that you fill
vacuity, say always yes always,
when the second moon in one month
breaks through clouds, shows itself all
day, that the rise of your nipples
at night, the silver chafing dish
on the table, when we are uncovered with
linen I want to say so, stay long inside
you that you might truly hear me say so,
that we might pick the ripe pear, eat it in
the afternoon, after sex, after no one is alive
but us, changed with the loud large
timpani of love, bathing afterwards, rubbing
and rubbing and rubbing ourselves clean, and
on the Persian rug in the study, where we
speak love to ourselves, the guests we
welcome as our bodies, hosts of love, and making
bread, its third rising, the cry that tells
us the bread is sliding up the sides of the slick
pan, and our hot fingers, our tongues telling all,
the hair we're twirling, curling in this furnace, and
now that you know again, your face loveliest, loveliest.

Without Which Not

Anything we see is seen by
us, the last long afternoon of great
sighs, the rocking of our bodies,
the quiver of joy that holds all

the arrows. We throw the mattresses
on the floor because the neighbors
complain of the loud springs, the louder
summers, the heat we make in internal

combustions, nearly busting out
the doors of this life into the pure sex
of pure love. That's our nature, the sound
of cream churning, the cha-cha, the undressing,

the sleight of hand, the great crash and
the greater rise. Bones pressed
to bones, skin to skin, lips to lips
to lips to lips. The invention of rhythm

as the world in us knows it. We grind
the colors for cave paintings,
holler the words the poets use:
Rub our legs, yes. Close our eyes, yes.

Climb inside, yes. Kiss our lips, yes.
Say the words, yes. Drink the breath, yes.
Touch the breast, yes. All the rest, yes.
Yes the yes, yes. Yes the yes, yes.

About the Author

Edward Kleinschmidt's first book of poems, *Magnetism*, won the Poetry Award from the San Francisco Bay Area Book Reviewers Association. His second, *First Language*, received the Juniper Prize; his third, *To Remain*, won the Gesu Award.

Kleinschmidt's poetry has appeared in *American Poetry Review*, *Gettysburg Review*, *Iowa Review*, *Massachusetts Review*, *New England Review*, *The New Yorker*, *Poetry*, *TriQuarterly*, *Virginia Quarterly Review*, and *The Best American Poetry*.

Recipient of a 1997 National Endowment of the Arts Poetry Fellowship, Edward Kleinschmidt teaches at Santa Clara University. He lives in San Francisco, California, and in Cortona, Italy. The poems in *Bodysong* were written over a period of fifteen years.

About the Book

Bodysong was designed and printed by Robin Heyeck using metal Centaur and Arrighi type on acid free Mohawk Letterpress paper. The edition was Smythe sewn and bound in paper wrappers by Cardoza James Bindery.